# SPIRITUAL ENERGY CYCLES

*Jackie Woods*

Adawehi Press

40 Adawehi Drive

Columbus, North Carolina 28722

Printed in the United States of America

Library of Congress Catalogue Card Number: 97-094141

ISBN: 0-9659665-0-X

*To Rodney*

# SPIRITUAL ENERGY CYCLES

Jackie Woods
with Russell Woods

Adawehi Press
Columbus, North Carolina 28722

# *Foreword*

Up to my neck in the accumulated issues of this life and, as I later came to appreciate, countless others, I first sought assistance from Jackie in 1984. Mistakenly assuming that healing was about "fixing symptoms," I thus began an eleven-year adventure of accelerated personal and spiritual growth as her client and student that has profoundly transformed my life. As a practicing healer, a gift she helped birth and as an academic with an abiding interest in healing practices worldwide, my time with her has been a singular blessing.

Perhaps the most fundamental lesson I integrated during my time with her is that the relationship between our inner worlds of consciousness and outer worlds of objective reality is the reverse of what our culture teaches. The world is not there to create struggle, victimize us, block our spiritual progress, or provide us with excuses for our unhappiness. It's there to provide a stage or medium through which all of the dramas of consciousness, from agony to ecstasy, can be expressed and properly reflected. Once one grasps this fundamental inversion, whether it manifests in the form of repressed anger crystallizing as a tumor, or as your boss failing to acknowledge your contributions at work, the door is open to many paths of growth. Without this realization, the chances of becoming stuck in places you don't want to be are significantly increased.

Jackie builds foundations first and towers later. It's not very glamorous at times. You can easily find other teachers who will "take you up" very quickly and create the illusion of rapid spiritual growth. Her work is more akin to building the foundations of a pyramid, taking as long as necessary to go all the way around the base before moving to the next level. You can, of course, erect flagpoles more quickly than pyramids; but flagpoles get blown over by the winds of change. Pyramids don't.

I always found that Jackie walks her talk. Everything she asks her students to do, or recommends for their consideration, she either does or has already done herself. This can include everything from honoring the physical body with daily exercise and healthy food (which many teachers do not) to journaling, advanced meditation, and appropriate role modeling in class. Most important, the growth challenges she helps students with she has for the most part experienced and worked with herself. With a vulnerability seldom seen in teachers who have "been around," Jackie grows with her students. She never quits. Accordingly, this book reflects a direct experiential knowing on many levels; it is not merely a series of theoretical reflections.

Jackie's spiritual gifts are so powerfully developed, yet gently applied, that attempts to describe them are doomed to fall short of the mark. Her ability to access past lives almost instantaneously, to evaluate and work with energy fields at a distance, to transmute material substances, to speak directly with archangels (and I do not mean this metaphorically), to connect a student to appropriate beings on his or her home planet, to remain subtly connected with all of her students at all times, to loosen the roots of negative emotions struggling for expression, to sense unhealthy or otherwise odd energies about a social gathering an hour before she arrives (which is why she avoids them), to enter your unconscious (with your prior permission) and "arrange" some dreams, plant some appropriate thought-forms, and clear out a few others, as well as to honor a few "night time requests" for planetary work by the Spiritual Hierarchy, in my opinion would stun even the most committed esotericist – if, that is, she ever talked about her gifts in a collective fashion, which she never does!

If there is an educational point to be made that requires an indirect reference to these gifts, she will do so. But only students who have been with her a number of years begin to sense the awesome range of her abilities in this arena. In an era when books extolling the wonders of medical clairvoyance and etheric surgery are gaining popularity, it is useful to remind ourselves that advanced souls most people never heard of have been doing such work for a long time.

One of the most effective and convenient aspects of Jackie's work is that, after a few years, you've either done or learned how to do many things that command special labels and otherwise many separate weekend workshops — whether it's breathwork, subtle body integration, dream analysis, inner child work, or meeting angelic guides. For example, most of her students do past life work when it is called for, never as a curiosity junket. However, they are not hypnotically regressed to past lives. Indeed, the few times I tried this with hypnotherapists, nothing much happened. By contrast, in my work with Jackie, I would simply close my eyes, take a few deep breaths, and begin to look at and interact with my "inner screen" which she not only was simultaneously monitoring, but also helping me to see in the first place. What helped make this process so efficient, I later learned, was that I had been "prepped" during my sleep and/or dream time the night before.

Jackie uses her gifts appropriately. But they are not what she is about. For they are anchored in a depth of spiritual connection and radiance that signals the emergence of a living master. This as much as anything, I believe, many of her students (myself included) unconsciously sense and seek out, even though they may not put words around it. Realized teachers may use certain gifts and not others. However, that is not what defines them. What defines them is the clarity of their emotional body and the radiance of their spiritual body, which is fully integrated both with Source and with one's other bodies, including the physical. Everything else is secondary. From a functional point of view, this means that typically they do not teach by doing, but simply by being – that is, by radiating their essence in an extensive field that instantly affects and often transforms the consciousness of all who come into it. With perfect discernment they listen, they see, and they illuminate the terrain with no more words than are necessary. What their students need on that day they provide with humor, grace, and compassion, even though it may not be recognized as such. Consciousness is subtly changed, but to an outsider it might appear as if nothing has happened. As I reflect upon all that Jackie overtly "does" with her students as well as the considerable responsibilities that she absolutely requires them to assume for their own growth, I know that she, too, is evolving toward honored pathways that only a few walk — where nothing is done, but everything is accomplished.

If I were to read my own reflections before I ever met Jackie, I might enter her space for the first time with a sense of anxiety or caution, not knowing what to expect. Yet for all that she is capable of as a healer and teacher, she comes across as a person in ways that belie the stereotypical expectations of aloofness or arrogance that society has created for teachers of her stature. She radiates a "down home" charm, a keen sense of humor, a zest for living, and a greater desire to exercise at the gym than to read another self-help book. She knows how to put you at ease and instantly does so. She'd rather learn a ballroom dance, or have a discussion about yard art, than listen to a panel of hot New Paradigm speakers. And whether you're a complete stranger or an old student, struggling in your darkest valley or just mowing the lawn, as her playful smile takes shape you get the sense that she's thanking you for the opportunity to dance in one of life's freshly created opportunities. Such, at least, has been my experience.

Universal teachings inevitably translate into different lessons and life streams for different students. What we do with our work thus contributes to the evolving spectrum of the universe that God is able to enjoy. For all that I learned and birthed in my work with Jackie, perhaps the most profound reminder — a universal constant whose resonance never dies —  is the heart-centered acknowledgment I felt in my connection with her. It's that way, I believe, in all authentic student-teacher relationships, where unconditional love transforms the path, reminds us of who we are, helps us to claim it, and forever points the way home.


Mark Woodhouse Ph.D.
Professor of Philosophy
Georgia State University

# Preface

For 18 years my mother, Jackie Woods, has been a spiritual healer and teacher. While I was growing up, I tried to distance myself from that whole world. I just wanted her to go back to being "Mom." I thought that all those who came to work with her were simply the kind of people that refused to take action. "If you want to stop smoking, just make up your mind and do it," was my attitude. I was of the opinion that anyone who proclaimed that they were into "New Age" things, was just someone who was into wishful thinking. "Saying 'bad things won't happen to me anymore' doesn't make it so" was my standard judgment of people trying to change their lives through the use of anything that fell under the heading of "Metaphysics." It was a dimly understood and dirty word for me.

However, by the time I graduated from massage school, four years ago, my world view had changed significantly. I would be giving someone a massage and I would feel a "shift." What had been rock-hard knots of muscle, would suddenly become smooth, relaxed tissue. As the tension released from their body, there would be a flood of emotion released with it. People would suddenly "see" where they were sabotaging their own lives. All this could not possibly be from the mechanical action of rubbing someone's back. Was this the shift in "energy" that I had grown up believing to be "New Age mumbo-jumbo?" If so, could it be applied to other areas of life than just release of physical tension? I decided to start taking the classes on Personal Growth that my mother was teaching.

Through these classes and workshops, and through my new-found commitment to working on myself, I began to see the outlines of an ongoing process and not just isolated breakthroughs or revelations. As I look back and see where my life is now, compared to where it was when I started, I'm amazed at the changes that I've been able to create in just about all aspects of my life. My career, the relationship between my wife and I, my enjoyment of life – all are better than I ever would have dreamed possible back then. I began to wish I could pass on this idea of personal growth as ongoing change, achieved by commitment to an understandable and cohesive process, or series of steps.

I still believe that many people who say they are into personal growth just like to "talk the talk" but don't carry their beliefs all the way through into actual change. For those who do want to enact changes, but don't know how, or just don't want to have anything to do with something that smacks of "hocus-pocus," (like I didn't), I decided to help my mother write a book.

I listened to hours of taped workshops and lectures that she had given, and tried to condense it all down into the basics a person would need to get started on their own path of personal growth and change. The basic process is very simple, but there are so many ways to trip yourself up that you could write ten books and not cover all the possibilities. I hope I have struck a balance between saying too little and confusing you with too much esoterica.

The Earth's frequency is speeding up and things that used to happen slowly and with little intensity are now hitting us fast and hard. The current spate of natural disasters and Earth changes that we see in the news everyday is proof of that. We won't be able to pull together collectively to live in this "New Age" (there's that damn word again!) if enough individuals don't decide to start on their own path of personal growth. Personal paths must lead away from fear and isolation toward the chance to bring personal power to bear on the problems that face us all. I hope that this book will provide clear, simple steps, that people can follow toward that end.

# Table of Contents

# 1

# *The Basics*

E=mc². Matter is really energy. Einstein's famous formula. We all pay lip service to this idea, but we don't really believe that the world works that way. Like the Surgeon General's warning in the corner of a cigarette ad, we see it, believe it absolutely, and then carry on as if it weren't part of the equation. Well, that's all metaphysics really is ... putting the idea that everything is energy into everyday use in your life. This book will explain how it all works and how you can use this idea to bring growth and change into your life.

Metaphysics is a vague and filmy concept that most of us don't know much about, but energy is familiar to us in many forms. It has many common properties that we can relate to from our knowledge of electricity, light, kinetic energy (the energy of motion), and all its many and various forms that we studied in eighth grade Physical Science. Several of these basic properties are as follows:

1. Energy has flow, usually cyclical. It wants to move. Example: electricity can't stand still; it exists only as an electrical current. In our energy fields we see this manifested as the external cycle of Giving and Receiving and the internal cycle of Growth and Manifestation. Both of these cycles will be examined in this book.

2. Energy has polarity: +/-, ying/yang, odd/even. In our energy fields, we see this manifested as Male and Female.

3. An energy field has magnetism - it draws like things to it. Examples: gravity, an electromagnet. This is how we create our own reality.

4. Energy seeks balance. Example: a bolt of lightning will always try to ground itself. We

will see that in our own energy fields, this balance will become external if there is no internal balance. For instance, a person who gets their sense of worth from taking care of others will usually end up marrying a person who wants to be taken care of.

Scientists will no doubt cringe at how I've played fast and loose with the laws of physics, and, to be sure, I have oversimplified things, but I think most laymen will agree that they have seen energy act in the ways described above.

So, there you go - everything is energy, and that's how energy works. Simple right? Well, maybe. I've made some statements above about how this plays out in our lives, but let's examine them in detail.

First, if everything is energy then **we** are energy. I've been referring to our "energy fields", but what does that mean? The physical form that we think of as our "body" is really four separate energy fields overlaid on top of each other. These four energy fields are the Physical, the Emotional, the Mental and the Spiritual. Each one is centered around a focused energy point called a "chakra." This means that there is a Physical chakra, an Emotional chakra, a Mental

chakra, and a Spiritual chakra. These four energy centers, or points, are sort of central "clearing
houses" for energy flowing through the Body
that they represent. That is to say that if, for
instance, there is going to be a blockage of energy flow, or "logjam," through the Emotional
Body, the Emotional chakra is probably where it
will first become evident. Since the Emotional
chakra is located just below the navel, this
blockage might manifest itself as a physical
tightening of the muscles in that area or even a
constriction in the digestive flow: i.e. a bout of
constipation.

There are seven major chakras, the four
"lower" chakras mentioned above, and the three
"higher" chakras: the power center in the throat,
the "third eye" in the forehead, and the crown
chakra on top of the head. The four lower
chakras are related to our physical reality, the
upper three are more attached to that part of us
that is independent of this present incarnation.
If you're religiously inclined you would probably
call that part "the soul."

All energies have a specific frequency or
vibration. For example, a specific frequency of
light would be a particular color; a specific frequency of sound would be a particular pitch or

note. So, a collection of energy fields at successively higher vibrations, as described above, is really just a spectrum. Your energy field is a spectrum, with each chakra being a specific frequency in that spectrum. Your "soul," or "higher self" – or whatever term you prefer – is the highest and most energetic frequency of that spectrum, and your physical matter is the lowest, densest, and slowest frequency. No surprise then, really, that an energy pattern expressed on one of the higher levels such as a prayer, could make a small change at one end of the spectrum, eventually percolating down into a lower vibration as a large, perceptible change. We will examine this Manifestation Cycle in some detail later in this book.

Do you remember Roy G. Biv? That was the acronym for the array of colors you got when you sent a beam of light through a prism in science class and it refracted into a rainbow. The acronym stands for **R**ed, **O**range, **Y**ellow, **G**reen, **B**lue, **I**ndigo, and **V**iolet. Anything that is energy has a specific rate of vibration (remember energy can't sit still); this is called its frequency. And if something has a frequency, then it has both a sound and a color. Only a very small portion of those frequencies fall into ranges in the two scales that our eyes and ears can pick up. Since our energy fields are a collection of different frequencies, like "white" light, they can also be broken down into these same colors. Red is at the bottom end of the rainbow because it has the lowest frequency (travels at the slowest vibration). So, the color red corresponds to our densest and slowest aspect: the Physical.

For those of you who are visually oriented, it may help to imagine the outline of a person, then color in each of our focused energy centers, or chakras, with its corresponding color. The chakra for the Physical body is at the base of the spine in the groin/tailbone region, and as I mentioned, it would be colored red. The Emotional chakra is located right below the navel in front of the sacrum bone of your spine; its color is orange. The Mental chakra is in the solar plexus right below the "wishbone" of your sternum; its color is yellow. The Spiritual chakra is in the center of the chest, in our "heart" space; its color is green. We have already touched on the other three: the throat chakra, which is our center of power and communication; the "third eye," or psychic center in our forehead; and our connection to our higher self – the "crown" chakra – at the top of our head. Their respective colors are: blue, indigo, and violet. *(Fig. 1)*

## The Seven Chakras Create Our Aura

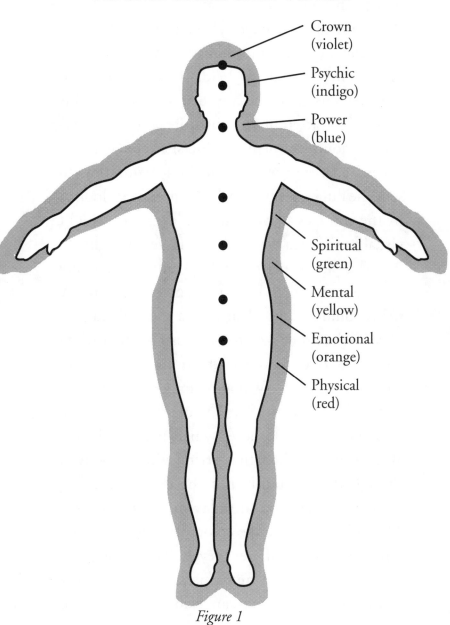

*Figure 1*

So when a psychic says they "see" a lot of orange in your "aura," what they really mean is that a lot of your energy is concentrated in the Emotional chakra, and they are sensing that lack of flow in your energy field. [Please note: as in the previous sentence, my use of "they" in this book is an attempt to substitute a gender-neutral pronoun for the hated "he/she" convention.] Likewise, if you wanted to do a meditation to send healing energy to a knot of anxiety lodged in the muscles of your solar plexus, you might visualize the area being bathed in yellow light.

What about corresponding sounds? Like any collection of ascending frequencies, our energy fields could also be likened to a musical scale. If you lift the lid of a piano, you can see that when you strike one C note all the other C strings up and down the scale will also vibrate slightly. This is called resonance. So, if your Physical chakra corresponds to a C note (which it does), it will also resonate when that string vibrates - even though it is certainly not the exact same frequency C that you are playing on the piano. This is how music, like color, can affect us powerfully on many different levels. This same principle of resonance helps us understand how changes on one level can lead to changes on another level - the "percolate down" effect to which I keep referring.

Chakras, Frequency, Color, Sound!! Wait!! Too much to keep track of. You're probably right. The important concept to grasp is that human beings are not just static lumps of matter. We are made of energy fields that affect, and are affected by, the rest of the world. Our energy fields have several different levels that interact with each other and our surroundings. Our physical bodies, then, are just the hard, innermost kernel of an onion-like energy field that floats in the sea of energy that makes up our reality. Is that better? At least for now, let's deal only with that idea and put names like "auras", "etheric and astral bodies", and any other metaphysical terms you may have heard, aside.

So, our bodies are nothing more than energy fields. Not so hard to believe. We all readily admit that matter is energy, and we are matter. If we are energy fields, then we exhibit the properties that energy does, right? If energy has to flow, then we have to flow. In fact, a healthy body is the manifestation of a flowing energy field. So a blocked or stagnant energy field would manifest as an injury or disease, right? Absolutely. An affliction of the physical body is caused by a block in our energy field, held in place by an emotion. Always. Sound like a strong statement? Why? If you made lemonade with stagnant water, the finished product would be rather "diseased" wouldn't it?

But what about dropping a hammer on your foot: how could that be caused by a block in your energy field? Well, if you hold your arm near the energy field of the television screen, the hairs all stand up. So you know that energy fields affect their environment. And we know that energy has this "magnetic" property. So what if your field contained the belief (an energy) that you couldn't stand up for what was rightfully yours, held in place by the fear of confronting your boss about a raise? Couldn't that magnetically draw an accident to the part of your body that symbolically represents standing?

OK, here's the keystone. If everything is energy, then God or the Universe or whatever your idea of perfection is, is also energy. So, as energy beings, we are all part of that perfection. We are all made of the same energy as the rest of the Universe (God included), so we are all connected. This is where the idea of Universal Oneness comes from which we have learned to associate with shaved-headed monks in some monastery in Tibet.

Now, when I say we are all made of the same energy, I am not trying to imply that we have no differences. For instance, the Atlantic and Pacific Oceans are obviously connected and, really, made up of the exact same water, but they have many different characteristics: direction of currents, frequency of storms, temperature, etc. Because they are different expressions of the same thing, we think of them as separate entities; as energy beings, we are the same way. If we accept this concept of connectedness, it makes it much easier to imagine that changes in our energy fields would lead to changes in the flow of energy that is creating the circumstances in our lives. After all, raising the water temperature in the Atlantic by even a few degrees would eventually affect the quantity and quality of marine life in the Pacific.

Obviously, in the earlier example about the raise and the hammer, it would be ludicrous for a being which is part of Perfection to not have the strength or the right to stand up for what they deserve. So, we see that a block in energy flow is really an Untruth. In fact, all the Untruths that end up as blocks in our energy fields –"I'm not good enough," "I can't get what I need," "I'll always be alone," etc. – are really

just variations of the central Untruth that we are
not part of that Perfection or God-Energy.
Nevertheless we hold these untruths in all four
of our bodies, Physical, Emotional, Mental, and
Spiritual, all the time, and the manifestation of
these blocks into our world causes us much pain
and suffering. In this book we are going to look
at how to change this process.

So, what I've been asserting here, in a rather
round-about way, is that we create our own reality. Whatever we are holding in our energy
fields, Truth or Untruth, flow or stagnation, is
what we create (manifest) in our life. Our energy
fields are the pattern or blueprint of what actually percolates down into the densest and lowest
energy level or vibration, the Physical reality
that we all know. For example: a person is holding an Untruth in their energy field (held in
place by fear) that says "When things are going
good for me, something bad always happens."
Well, this person just got a raise at work. Guess
what? They try to make a left hand turn through
traffic, and the person going the other way just
happens to be holding an Untruth in **their** energy field (held in place by guilt) that says "I'm
not a trustworthy person." Sure enough, this
person is driving a car that they borrowed from

their mother. You see where this is going, right? If an accident happens: is it Fate, predestination, Will of God, random coincidence, or two corresponding energy fields working together to draw in a situation that will play out both of those beliefs? Obviously, I'm going to lobby for the latter position. Not really a radical stand to make, if you go back to the belief that the very fabric of the universe is energy first and matter second. A situation being drawn together and created by energy is not hard to imagine, if you accept that the energy is where it starts and that matter is only an afterthought...the last to get the message. If a structure has already been set up on a higher vibration of the energy spectrum, the physical matter or actual happening is just the end result.

Now, neither of the people in the above example consciously chose to get in an accident. It is therefore very easy to take the role of Victim rather than "own up to" our position as Creators of our own reality. These Untruths can be very deeply buried in our unconsciousness, and yet, since they are still in our energy field, they are helping to form the blueprint from which we create our reality. A very powerful, but not very attractive, concept. Much simpler to chalk it up to "bad luck" and take the other guy to court. Taking that position, however, means that those unconsciously held (and Untrue) beliefs will continue to play out in our lives. Understanding how to bring these blocks out into the light and heal them is addressed in Chapter 3, the Growth Cycle.

The analogy of a river is a useful mental picture to help us visualize this process of energy flow creating our reality. The general shape and course of the river stays pretty constant as you look at it from minute to minute (although it does change in the long run, of course), but the water running past you at any given minute is not the same water that was there the minute before. That particular batch is now quite aways downstream. Our energy fields are the same way. When everything is going as it should, we are merely the completion of a circuit that connects us to our Higher Self, the Universe, or whatever you like to call that which is greater than us. So it is the pattern that the energy flows through, and not the actual energy, that forms what we see.

These "patterns" that channel the energy are our beliefs about who we are and how the world works. Although on some level we hold them to be gospel, these beliefs may, as we have seen, bear precious little resemblance to the real Truth: we are all part of the same energy as God or Perfection, and all the corollaries which follow from that. To carry the analogy further, we, like the river, must have flow. If part of the river's current gets diverted from its Perfection (onward flow), that water forms a stagnant pool or eddy. Mosquitoes begin to breed there. Sticks, garbage, and other flotsam begin to build up, and soon a logjam or block is formed. We are the same way. If we are holding a pattern that deviates from our Truth of Perfection, then we get blocked and stagnant places in our energy field soon begin to manifest as physical disease, accidents, or maybe just "diseased" life situation patterns (Why do I keep attracting relationships with people who are afraid of commitment?).

A Flowing energy field is a healthy energy field, but aside from the blocks that we are trying to get rid of in this book, our energy fields are sometimes cluttered with other things: mental chatter, stray emotions that aren't stuck ...we just forgot to let go of them, even unacknowledged physical needs (Hey, my stomach has been rumbling for the last ten minutes but I've been so wrapped up in this project that I didn't pay attention!). It helps to get this energetic "clutter" out of the way before trying to deal with our deep-seated programming, or blocks. Meditation is an ideal tool for clearing ourselves in preparation for this process. The next chapter will outline some ways to use meditation in helping to establish the two energies of *Flow\** and *Balance.*

*\*Throughout the book italicized words refer to heart energies. Further explanation on page 35.*

# 2

## *Flow and Balance*

If everything is energy, then breathing in and out is certainly a flow of energy. Much like taking a deep breath helps to calm you when receiving bad news or how a woman in labor is asked to "breath into the contraction," the breath is a very effective way you can physically do something to move energy.

Thoughts would also be energy. Visualization is a common practice with successful athletes. They will often picture in their minds the exact sequence of the task they are getting ready to perform, thereby adding energy to the nerve pathways that will soon carry out that action. For these reasons, Breath and Visualization are two of the most powerful tools for doing a clearing meditation so that flow can be maintained in your life.

To demonstrate their effectiveness, I would like to offer a sample meditation. Certainly, there are no rules for meditation. If the procedure I outline below doesn't work for you, do not feel constrained to follow it. I am merely trying to give an example of how these two tools, Breath and Visualization, can be used to make a meditation more effective.

Begin by closing your eyes and making yourself comfortable, either lying down or sitting with both feet flat on the floor. Next, turn your attention to the Breath. Breathe by allowing your diaphragm to drop and your abdomen to expand, **not** by trying to expand your chest. As you continue this "tummy breathing," let your attention follow the air in and out. When your breathing has become deep and regular, visualize your Physical chakra at the base of your tailbone. Breathe down into it and let the Breath expand it like blowing on the embers of a fire. See its Red color grow brighter and brighter. It may seem to get big in a hurry or it may stay relatively small. That's okay. Let it be however it needs to be...don't force it. As the Breath activates this Physical chakra, begin to feel it resonate throughout your Physical energy field (Body). Let physical tensions flow out with the out-going breath. Feel your shoulders and other chronic tension areas relax. Let your Physical body speak to you. "I'm hungry." "This seat cushion feels lumpy." Acknowledge each of these voices and then let them go. Breathe them out.

When the Physical chakra feels fully activated, and each of its voices has been heard and allowed to release, let the Breath draw the energy up to your second chakra, the Emotional. See it as a ball of energy located just below your navel. Breathe into this point of light which is the center of your Emotional body and let it expand, its Orange color getting brighter and brighter. Let any Emotional voices that need to speak, be heard. "I'm still mad at my sister-in-law for that cheap birthday gift." "I'm worried about all the bills this month." Don't try and fix them, just acknowledge that they are there and let them go. See them float up and out with the Breath. If one screams for attention, reassure it that you will come back to it later and let it float on out so that your Emotional space can be clear.

When the Emotional chakra feels fully activated, and each of its voices has been heard and allowed to release, let the Breath draw the energy up to your third chakra, the Mental. See it as a glowing point of energy in your solar plexus, just below your "wishbone." As you visualize the Yellow color of this chakra, feel the energy field of the surrounding Mental body begin to quiet down. Let each of the stray thoughts that come up flow across your internal screen and off the other side. Acknowledge them, but don't let them draw you into conversation. "I wonder if I cleaned out my In-box at work?" "Are we having meatloaf for lunch?" Breath them up and out, clearing the space.

When each of the three lower Bodies have been cleared and activated, turn your attention to the Heart chakra, the center point of your Spiritual Body. Visualize it in the center of your chest as a Green spark of energy. Breathe into it and see how the Breath connects it to the lower three chakras like pearls on a string. As the Spiritual body is cleared and activated like the lower three, with each of its voices being acknowledged and released, let the Breath strengthen the ribbon of energy that connects them all. Feel it grow into a pole of light that runs all the way through the center of your body. Let any cares or sorrows that are weighing heavy on your heart be whisked up and out by this rushing river of energy.

Complete the process by extending this shaft of energy up through your neck and out through the top of your head, clearing and activating the three upper chakras along the way: the blue Throat chakra in your neck; the indigo colored Psychic chakra, or "Third Eye," in your forehead; and the violet colored Crown chakra at the top of your head. See once again how they are all connected like pearls on a string by the stream of energy that now runs all the way through you. Feel how this beam of light connects you through your feet to the Earth and through the crown of your head to that which is greater (God, Higher Self, whatever you are comfortable with).

Your energy field is now clean and flowing, "seal the deal" by visualizing an egg-shaped envelope of pure white light that surrounds you and prevents outside energies from flowing into the internal spaces you have created. Take a few more deep, clearing breaths to finish your meditation and open your eyes.

Once again, the meditation I have just outlined is **not** the only way to establish flow in your energy field. Many people incorporate

movements, such as in Tai-chi, or sounds, such
as chanting. Personal preference should be the
guiding force in choosing how to meditate. But
regardless of the form it takes, meditation can be
a valuable tool. It can help you release the "static," the random energy that is cluttering up your
energy field. In this way, you can start with a
"blank slate" as you prepare to tackle those deep-
seated patterns which are blocking your Growth.

When used regularly, meditation can move
beyond being just a tool for clearing and activating your energy field. Once those "housekeep-
ing" activities have been performed, you can
begin to use meditation as a kind of "micro-
scope" to examine where the energy is flowing
(or not) in your energy field, and consequently
your life; or to see where the energy is out of
balance. Your life is out of balance when too
much is going out and not enough is coming in.
Your life is out of balance when too much is
moving down and not enough moving up.

From the River analogy, we've already seen
how lack of Flow can be caused by programmed
patterns which are not an expression of our true
selves. Now that we have the tool of Meditation
to point these places out, it is high time we
stopped talking about these patterns and started

changing them. This happens through the Growth Cycle. We will examine that in the next chapter, but first, let me make one final digression. We need to talk about the other major area where Meditation can help you spot a problem. We touched on it briefly a few sentences ago: it's called Balance.

Lack of Flow is just one of the ways that we can sabotage ourselves. Like any other form of energy, we can get out of balance. Too much Ying, not enough Yang...Too much detail, not enough Heart. This can also unintentionally cause us to create undesirable things in our reality. Like electricity, our energy field exhibits both a positive and a negative – a male and a female. Just like the electrical current, the positive and negative aspects of our energy fields need to be in balance.

Active/passive, giving/receiving, outgoing/ introspective, left-brained and linear versus right-brained and abstract. All of these dualities that we encompass in our make-up are attributes of our male and female energies striving for dominance.

Regardless of your sex, you have both a masculine and feminine side to your energy field. *(Fig. 2)* The Physical and Mental bodies are

## Male/Female Balance

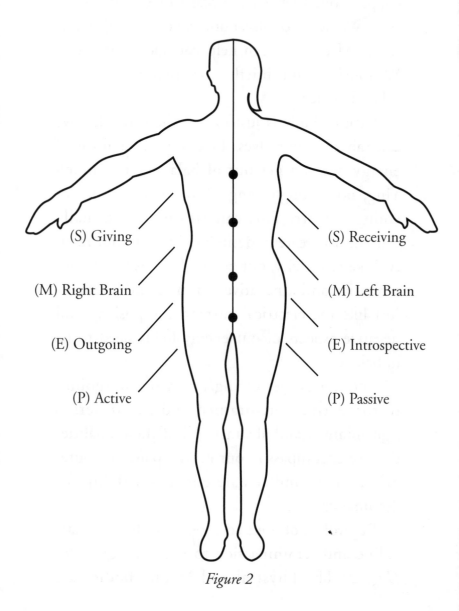

*Figure 2*

aspects of the male energy, while the Emotional and Spiritual correspond to the female side. Both male and female energies must play an equal and balanced part if we are to create smoothly. For example, a scientist who is very into his male energy and lives entirely in the concrete world of "what can be proven," may not have a blocked energy flow, but by being entirely divorced from the feminine world of the abstract, he is missing the beauty of the very things he is trying to understand. Surely, this is not very powerful creating. This is not a healthy and balanced energy system fulfilling all its own needs. Sadly, our male and female parts often do not work together, and are, in fact, openly antagonistic at times. The issues of gender inequality that we see played out in our society are the result. (Yes, if we each create our individual reality, collectively we create our society.)

We must resolve the war between the male and female energies. We've gone through history with matriarchy or patriarchy. It is time for an age of Balance. Only when we achieve internal balance will we be at one with our external world. Everything that is happening in our society today, everything that's manifesting, is a direct result of what's happening internally with people. For example, child abuse is suddenly a hot topic. We see news articles on it all the time.

Programs to teach children to say "No" are proliferating. It is not out of the ordinary to hear people openly admitting they were abused as a child. Certainly the abuse is not a new thing, but you never used to see signs of it in our culture. The reason it looms large in our collective consciousness and conventions of our society is that enough individuals have done their internal work to break the cycle. Their parents had an internal imbalance of discipline (masculine energy) and nurturing (feminine energy). They expressed it externally by hurting their kids, but the kids refused to pass it on.

Let's turn our attention now to how we can achieve these ideals of Flow and Balance. It all starts by becoming aware of, and then reprogramming the blocks or Untruths that we are holding in our energy fields. This is called the Growth cycle.

# 3

## *The Growth Cycle*

Needs are energy too, just like everything else. When we say "I need to be in a relationship," what we really mean is "I need the energies of *commitment* and *sharing* which I allow myself to receive in a relationship setting." Likewise, "I need money right now" really means "I need the energy of *abundance* that money represents for me." All these "things" that we think we need in order to be fulfilled and happy, can really all be boiled down to a specific energy or energies.

So where can these magical energies be found? Well, think. If we, as energy beings, are cut from the same cloth (so to speak) as God/Perfection/the All of the Universe, then all those various energies are to be found in us just as they are to be found in God. We have all those energies inside us, but we have to learn how to access them and use them so that we can begin to manifest all the "things" we need.

Haven't you, at some point in your life, known a person who had no "money issues"? If they needed $12,000, then some rich uncle they hardly knew died and left them exactly that amount. Or without even asking for it, they were promoted into a better paying job just as they were pondering building an addition onto their house? Whatever this person needs just seems to come to them. Why? Well, it's because they have learned, on some level, the Truth that they are able and deserving to hold the energy of *abundance* in their energy field and let it magnetically draw to them what they need. Great – why can't you do this? You can! If you are not doing it already, it is because somewhere in your energy pattern you are holding an Untruth that covers up your access to the energy of *abundance.* Finding these Untruths, which block our access to the energies that we need, is what the Growth Cycle is all about. Every time you claim one of these energies as your own, you Grow (expand your energy field). If you were ever able to claim all the possible energies, then you would have Grown to the point of Perfection/Oneness with God/Nirvana.

So what is the process by which we discover these blocks and Grow beyond them? The process is twofold: first, having an awareness of a need that is going unmet, and secondly, uncovering the Untruth which is blocking our access to the energy that we really need. Only after we have seen the Untruth for the lie that it is, can we claim our real need: the energy inside us which the Untruth was obscuring.

The first part is the province of our Emotional body. Emotional pain and distress are just little red flags that say "Warning: you have a need that is not being met." All of our four Bodies – Physical, Emotional, Mental and Spiritual – play a role in the Growth Cycle, and a somewhat reversed role in the corresponding Manifestation Cycle – but we are getting a bit ahead of ourselves there. *(Fig. 3)*

In the Growth Cycle, our emotions serve as our teachers. In any situation, if you have a need that is not being met, you will have an emotion. Period. Some of us are not very good at listening

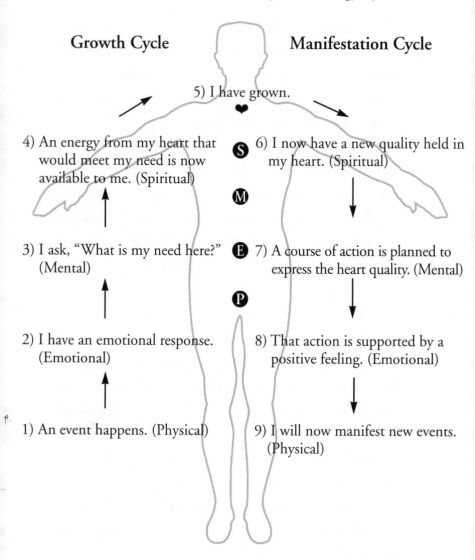

**Growth Cycle**                              **Manifestation Cycle**

5) I have grown.

4) An energy from my heart that
would meet my need is now
available to me. (Spiritual)

6) I now have a new quality held in
my heart. (Spiritual)

3) I ask, "What is my need here?"
(Mental)

7) A course of action is planned to
express the heart quality. (Mental)

2) I have an emotional response.
(Emotional)

8) That action is supported by a
positive feeling. (Emotional)

1) An event happens. (Physical)

9) I will now manifest new events.
(Physical)

*Figure 3*

to the voice of the Emotional body, but it always has something to say. For example, if someone capitalizes on my idea at work and reaps praise from the boss that I feel should rightfully have been mine, I may feel anger. That emotion, in this case anger, is trying to tell me that I have a need going unmet. That's all. Not that I should stab my co-worker with a ball point pen, but simply that somehow I was not receiving the energy that I needed from that interaction. Maybe the energy was *honor*. We can't be certain until we follow the Growth Cycle all the way through. But we're getting ahead of ourselves again. As another example, lets take the same situation described above but this time let's suppose that the emotion I experienced was fear. I became afraid that my co-worker would appear much smarter and more efficient to my boss and that I would soon be out of a job. Certainly, there is a different need not being met here. An energy other than *honor* was missing. That's why the emotion is there – a little red flag put there **by** me and **for** me. A guide to get me started on the path towards finding out what I'm not getting. Or suppose the co-worker was a friend and the emotion I felt was betrayal. Once again, the emotion is not there to remind me to hate my co-worker forever. Instead, it is there to bring to my attention the fact that for some reason I am not holding, in my energy field, the energy necessary to magnetically draw in what I need. I will need to work all the way through the Growth Cycle to find out what that reason may be.

Like a good teacher should, our emotions act as cheerleaders. If a particular situation is working for us and our needs are getting met, we will generate a "positive" emotion: happiness or excitement, for example. Most of us don't mind listening to those. However, if our needs are not being met, we will have pain. Emotional pain at first, (fear, guilt, anger and grief, to name a few) but if we push it away and do not let it express on that level, it will eventually percolate down the spectrum into physical pain. Unfortunately, we often let the situation get to this extreme. This is why chiropractors and massage therapists do such a booming business.

Our job then, is to listen to our emotional pain and see where it takes us. The biggest obstacle to this is owning our emotions. We must constantly remind ourselves that "this emotion is **for me and about me.**" If we fall into the Victim role of believing that "you made me angry," (or sad, or upset, etc.) or "you caused my pain," then all is lost. We will never get to the bottom of our feeling because we just gave it away. If you caused me to be angry, then it is not my anger, it is yours. If you yell at me, I can feel any one of a number of things, ranging from annoyance that you interrupted my chain of thought, to elation that you finally got that off your chest and now the air is clear. If I end up feeling angry about the yelling, it is because I **chose** that feeling from a wide range of possibilities. And that is the key, right there, for if I chose that feeling, there is a reason. The next question is automatically, "Why?" But if you **made** me angry, the line of questioning stops right there. Staying with our emotions about a particular situation long enough to own them and following them to the "Why" is the first step in the Growth Cycle.

The door to awareness is through the emotions. But many people get stuck in the doorway. They may feel and even express their feelings but never make it through the issue that is hiding who they are. Behind every feeling is a piece of you saying "I want to express." Not "I want to tell them off," but "I want to express **me for me.**" Life really is all about you! Many feelings are uncomfortable enough that we want to make the pain go away as quickly as possible. So we take a little taste of them and then quickly shove them back down, or onto someone else. This doesn't move them out of the way, and we don't get to the issue (the "Why") that is behind the feeling. However, if we can stay with the emotion long enough – not judging it, not pushing it away, just sitting right in the middle of it – then it begins to detach itself from the situation or other person and begins to reveal something about us. Instead of "you made me angry by yelling at me," it becomes "when you yelled, I became angry because _____." That empty blank is our "Why" and we may have to repeat that statement over and over to ourselves, letting that blank space just hang there, but eventually something will come up to fill it. When it does, we have our answer. "When you yelled, I became angry because...I was scared and my anger feels protective to me."

There may be several layers to our answer, but we keep asking "why" until we get to the rock bottom. You'll know you've reached the bottom when all you have left is a statement about who you are. Why did I get scared when you yelled? Because "I don't feel safe when other people express themselves with intensity." There! Rock bottom. A statement about who I am. I am a person who lacks the energy of *safety* in this situation. If you have really uncovered the issue behind your emotion, there will always be an energy missing. Remember, that is what the emotion is about – a need going unmet – and needs are energies, not "things".

Once you have stayed with the emotion long enough to detach it from the circumstances and get to the "Why," the second step is to replace the Untruth ("I lack *safety*") with your Truth ("I am made of the same energy as Perfection, I most certainly do have the energy of *safety* in me, and I can bring it to bear in any situation I choose").

Easy enough to say, but how do we put that into practice? Where do we find these Truths? Well, I said that all four of our bodies play a role in this process, but so far we've concentrated on only three: the Physical (the actual event – the yelling), the Emotional (being aware of the feelings), and the Mental (holding focus for long enough to get to the rock bottom). So that leaves the Spiritual body. Our spirit is the sum total of all the qualities that make us up: our *compassion,* our *love,* our sense of *adventure* and *play,* our capacity for *sharing,* to name only a few. So when we say "I am made of the same energy as Perfection and I do have the energy of *safety* in me somewhere" – that somewhere is our Spiritual body, centered in our Heart chakra. In fact, since we are made of the same energy, our Spiritual body contains all the same qualities (energies) as God/Perfection. The problem is that we have not claimed very many of those energies as our own. We generally are hanging on to a multitude of Untruths that assert such things as "I can not have *safety.*"

If the first step of the Growth Cycle, then, is Awareness of your need; the second step we will call "claiming your truth." The process is simple. It involves "tuning in" to your Spiritual body, just like you did with your Emotional body, to get to the need. If you can listen to your Emotional body, then you can also access your Spiritual body. It may take some practice, though, because many of us are not used to listening to that spiritual voice. It might be helpful to focus your consciousness there by breathing into the Spiritual (Heart) chakra. (Remember? Center of the chest, green in color.) When you have found that Spiritual space, speak the need into it. "I need *safety.*" Instantly, you will feel the energy of *safety* being drawn out of the very fabric of that Heart Space. It was there all along. The removal of the block (Untruth) and the introduction of the need simply allowed it to pop to the surface. Now claim that energy. "I am part of the energy of Perfection/God, and I **do** have the energy of *safety* in me and can call it forth whenever I choose." Claiming an energy may not do us much good if we can't find it again when we need it. If you have never had *safety* in your life before, the energy may feel unfamiliar and elusive. Part of the process then, is sitting in the middle of that energy, just like you did the emotion, until you know the feel of it inside and out. Until you know the "personality" of it so well that you can describe it in its elemental form – as an energy – not just how it plays out in your life. When you can do that, **then** you can call on that energy whenever you need it, and only then will you have really claimed it as a part of yourself. When we claim a new part of ourselves in this way, we have expanded our energy field. This is true Growth.

As an exercise, it may be useful to go back through your day (or week) and bring to mind situations in which you were aware of a strong emotional response. Then go through the

Growth Cycle process with each one (Hint: the steps are summarized in the next paragraphs). Ask yourself: Was I able to get clear on what the feeling was, or did it seem muddled? Perhaps a clearing meditation is in order. Was I able to detach the emotion from the situation, or did I "make it about them"? Did I get to the "Why" behind my emotion. Was it a clear statement of who I am in that situation? Did I complete the process by taking the need to my Spiritual body and claiming the energy there? By repeating this exercise with as many situations as you can think of, you will begin to get a clearer picture of where the process usually breaks down for you. If you simply can't get clear on a particular situation, don't obsess. Let it go and try another one. Practice makes perfect. Each time you successfully get all the way through the process it becomes that much easier to go back and work out one you are stuck on.

How can the claiming of an energy in our Spirit create safety in our actual day-to-day world? Will we really feel safe the next time someone yells at us? Stay tuned! The "creating the reality" portion of the process is dealt with when we examine the Manifestation Cycle. But first, a quick recap...

The easiest way to summarize the Growth

Cycle is to follow the process through each of our four Bodies. First, there is the **Physical:** an event happens – someone yells at us, for instance. Our job: be Aware. Is this really about me? What are my reactions?

Then there is the **Emotional:** How do I feel about this? What emotion am I holding around this event? Our job: own the emotion - don't let it stay attached to the outside world. Move from "you **made** me upset" or "I'm angry **at** you," to "I chose to become angry because ____."

Next there is the **Mental:** What is my need here? What is the "Why" behind my emotion?

Our job: stay focused through all the layers of "Why" until we get to the need at the rock bottom....the statement of who we are around that event.

Finally, there is the **Spiritual:** what energy or heart quality could I incorporate into my field that would meet this need? Our job: claim the energy by getting to know it thoroughly.

If you visualize this progression as a flow chart through our four Bodies and their corresponding Chakras, you will notice that the flow of this cycle is upward. The Growth Cycle is about following the energy of a situation up from the lowest and densest vibration of our spectrum to the highest and most energetic. This may seem like swimming upstream, but "earning it" in this way is what makes this physical reality such a powerful learning laboratory for us.

You will probably also notice that the Male aspects of our energy field, the Physical and Mental, play a rather passive role in the Growth Cycle – Awareness and Focus. Our Female side provides the activity during this part of the cycle – the Discovery of our Need (Emotional) and the Claiming of our Truth (Spiritual). If our Male and Female aspects are out of balance, we can get stuck at some point in the process and just keep repeating one segment instead of Growing beyond it. For example, if a person is most comfortable in their Mental body and allows that Body to be overactive and try and take charge (Male energy out of balance), they may not be able to maintain a focus long enough to get through all the layers of emotion and find the real need. If that is the case, the Cycle stops right there and the same issue keeps coming up in the person's life. They continue to have the same emotional reactions and get discouraged that they can't seem to break out of this pattern.

So, once again the twin pitfalls of Flow and

Balance come into play. If we are not hitting on all cylinders in one of these areas, how can we improve? Well, each time we do the process successfully, we get stronger in our internal connections and each part of us gets a better grasp on what its correct role is supposed to be. If you are having trouble, try to focus on each Body individually, step by step. Is each one doing its job? Is that Body being active or passive? For example, if your Physical response is to "do something" or "fix the situation" before you can even be with the emotion and get to the need, then the Physical body is too active and is probably getting in the way of your Awareness. Calm it down. Go back to the beginning of our Growth Cycle flow chart and do the first step again: just try and be aware.

# 4

# *The Manifestation Cycle*

Growth and Manifestation are actually all one cycle. Manifesting is just bringing into being the new expression of who we are...which we just uncovered in the Growth Cycle. These two processes are going on simultaneously and are feeding off each other. For example, what usually happens is that we will learn a small piece of who we are, Manifest that piece, and that will lead us to a new lesson or another aspect of the same lesson that we didn't get the first time through.

When I say "lesson," that is simply my term for a situation that we draw to us (Manifest) to provide an opportunity to uncover a new piece of who we really are (Grow). See now why it is called a Cycle? Why do we "draw things to ourselves"? Because the blueprint for them is in our energy field. Remember? The subconsciously held belief (Untruth), "I am not enough," creates the physical reality of Lack: not enough money, time, love, or any of the other "necessities."

**How** we do this is what the Manifestation Cycle is all about. We have already stated that we are energy and energy has a "magnetic" attraction to it, so if we claim a new energy, such as *abundance,* and hold that in our field, we will **automatically** begin to attract situations where we get what we need, rather than ones where we have Lack. Right? Yes, we would, if we could just stay out of our own way. Unfortunately, just like its counterpart, the Growth Cycle, the Manifestation Cycle contains many opportunities for us to block our Flow or get out of Balance.

Let's run through the individual steps, as we did with the Growth Cycle, so we can see where breakdowns might occur. First, the **Spiritual** body holds the new energy that we have claimed in our Growth (*safety, abundance, love* and *allowing,* to name a few examples). Second, the

**Mental** body begins coming up with ideas and possible structures that will allow us to express this new piece of who we are. For example, "What if I set a boundary of only bringing up this subject with people who can support me in it?" Third, the **Emotional** body, our cheerleader, provides us with an emotion, or emotions, that will get behind these new structures and push or add impact - for instance, the emotion of excitement. Finally, this new quality, through whatever forms or vehicle we have chosen, is brought out into our **Physical** reality.

If, for instance, the Spiritual body is weak and not doing its job, it will not hold the new quality, and the Mental body will go right on spinning out plans and schemes and possible reactions based on the old Untruth. The other bodies, if they are doing their jobs, will faithfully get behind these blueprints and carry them out, not knowing that they are continuing to create the same old patterns that didn't meet the need in the first place. Once again, Balance. All our bodies must pull their share of the weight. Or, what if the Flow is blocked in the Emotional body by a stuck emotion relating to an event that happened last week? If we can't move through that feeling, the emotions that we generate won't have anything to do with this new quality that we are trying to manifest, and once again, the process breaks down right there.

How do we correct this? How do we strengthen a Body we are weak in? How do we check to make sure we are not stuck somewhere? In both cases the answer is: spend more time focusing there. Try an exercise like the one we did for the Growth Cycle. Go back through your day and find situations where you felt you had a handle on what your need was and yet couldn't seem to manifest it into reality. Try to break each situation down into the individual steps outlined above. Focus on each Body at a time. Is your Spiritual body holding the energy or, do you, perhaps, not know the energy (quality) inside and out yet? Is your Mental body creating structures and boundaries that adequately express and protect this new quality in you? Is your Emotional body creating positive emotions to support this new quality or is it stuck in an old pattern? Do you have the Physical skills to carry out the forms of expression that your Mental is creating?

When you've identified a weak point...spend some time there. You could start by meditating and using your tools of Visualization and

Breathing to add strength and energy to a particular Body, but don't stop there. Spend time using the Body that needs strengthening. For instance, if your Mental body is not used to creating new ideas, give it some practice. Take a creative writing course, practice brainstorming, build a fantasy house in your mind, or make up secret names for all your friends based on their personalities and write them down in your journal. Try similar exercises for your other Bodies. If your stamina is not good, you can't expect it to improve by sitting around the house – you have to spend some time being Physical, working out at the gym for instance. Likewise, learning to hold a new quality in your Spiritual body requires that you spend some time focusing on that Body, through meditation or your own method, to get in touch with that part of yourself. The more time you spend consciously working through this Cycle, step by step, the stronger each part of you will get in doing its own job and the more you will recognize when and where the process is breaking down.

You will probably have noticed that everything is now reversed in the Manifestation Cycle. The flow of energy is now from the top (Spiritual) to bottom (Physical) of our energy spectrum – the opposite of the way it was during the Growth Cycle. Also, the Mental and Physical bodies now play the active roles of imagining and carrying out, while the Spiritual and Emotional bodies are relegated to the more passive roles of holding and encouraging.

Let's go back now and follow the process through from start to finish. While explaining the Growth Cycle, I gave the example of a person getting yelled at (Physical), feeling the anger and the underlying fear (Emotional) attached to that event, staying focused (Mental) long enough to work through the layers of emotion and get to the need for the energy of *safety* (Spiritual). I then posed the questions: "How can the claiming of an energy in our Spirit create safety in our actual day to day world? Will we really feel safe the next time someone yells at us?" So let's continue that example through the rest of the Cycle and see how that would work.

A person who has claimed the energy of *safety* gets yelled at. Instead of generating fear, and a covering layer of anger, based on the Untruth "I can't have safety," this person now holds *safety* in their heart (Spiritual chakra). So when the Mental body asks "Who am I in this situation?" the Spirit says "you deserve to and can be safe."

The Mental body then plans a course of action to express that sense of safety. Instead of reacting defensively or being paralyzed into inaction, as was the old pattern, it sets up boundaries and structures to create a safe environment: "I don't appreciate and won't tolerate being yelled at, and if that is the only way you can communicate, this conversation is over." The Emotional body also falls into line behind this new Spiritual focus; instead of generating fear, it creates a positive emotion, such as calm, to reinforce and lend resolve to the boundaries set by the Mental. The Physical body then chimes in with its strength and stamina to carry out whatever course of action has been chosen to express this new part of who we are, be that leaving the room or whatever.

What is the difference between this and just willing yourself not to be afraid - the power of "positive thinking" as it were? The difference is that when you are manifesting a new part of yourself that you have claimed, it actually **feels** different. If you are simply letting your mind repeat over and over "I'm not afraid, I can have safety," then your emotions are either being suppressed or are working at cross purposes and are generating the fear that tells you "there is still a need not being met here."

I have a friend who used to make me furious. He was always going on and on about how "if I was really serious about what we were undertaking together, I would do so and so." I always retorted angrily that **he** was the one whose actions didn't seem to show that he was serious. I was eventually able to work through this situation and get to my need. At our next meeting, I was holding the energy of *commitment* in my heart and, although he started in with the same old rhetoric, I felt no need to respond. I checked in with my Spiritual body and stood fast in the "knowing" (my word for awareness beyond Mental knowledge) that *commitment* **was** part of who I was – no matter what he said. The words were the same as always, but this time they didn't affect me. I had moved to a different place. When we claim a new quality as part of ourselves, we really do become a different person. The Manifestation Cycle is just the expression into the world of this change that has already taken place on a higher level of our energy spectrum.

Ok, Ok. I can already hear the next question: I am beginning to see how a new energy or quality that I hold in my energy field (specifically in my Spiritual "Heart" chakra) could change the way I view the world and might make me react differently, **but** can it change the outside world? What if my need is for *love* or *abundance?* How can holding those energies make my wife open up her heart to me or my boss give me more money? Well, to answer those questions fully, we need to examine our last big Cycle: The Giving and Receiving Cycle.

# 5

## *The Giving and Receiving Cycle*

Whenever we hold a particular energy (heart quality) in our field, that energy flows out in everything we do. As it flows out, it leaves behind a Space, a vacuum. And Nature abhors a vacuum! This vacuum creates the magnetic pull that draws that energy back to us to meet our need, although not necessarily from the same source to which we gave. This out-going energy expresses into our Physical world in various concrete vehicles or Forms such as our actions, or the way we are in the world, for example. These energies also come back to us in Forms, but the

Form and the Energy behind it should not be confused. If we have not gone through the Growth process to claim this quality as part of us, we may **think** we are broadcasting it, but there is no real energy behind it. We can say: "I'm a generous person; I believe in abundance – Look, I just gave all the change in my pocket to that Salvation Army person standing outside the store." But if the real reason we gave was from a sense of obligation, whether we admit this consciously or not, then there was no energy of *abundance* behind that form and it will not flow back to us as abundance. It was probably just wasted effort; because, while it looked just like abundant giving would, it was an empty Form.

In fact, if we gave from a place of obligation (a mental judgment, not a Heart quality), then there was no movement or flow of energy and our Giving didn't leave behind it a space. So, there was no space for anything to flow back into and we didn't really enter into the Giving and Receiving Cycle. Even if the Salvation Army person said "Thank you" and expressed the energy of *gratitude,* there was no space for us to receive it. What we give without receiving is wasted, a drain on our energies, and what we receive without giving has no power and no movement. Giving and Receiving really should be thought of as pieces of the same thing.

Let's step back for a moment to make sure the Big Picture is still there. Are you still having problems with the idea that energy and matter are the same thing? Do you doubt that an energy flowing into a space in our energy field is really going to translate as a physical need getting met - actual food for our table or clothes on our back? If so, why? Remember, $E=mc2$. Everything is energy. The energy behind a particular action, say the designing of a house, is as real as the concrete matter of the architect's drawing that is the end result. In fact, if the energy didn't exist first, the action would never have been contemplated or carried out. So, by Giving out the energy of *abundance,* we create a space in our energy field that is like a lock looking for a key - a magnetic lock **drawing** to it the key which is the exact fit. The exact fit would be someone needing to express their Truth just as you needed to express *abundance.* In this situation, it might be your boss expressing her Truth of *gratitude* by giving you a raise. So by creating that space, you created extra money in your paycheck as surely as if you had written the check yourself.

We are conditioned to believe that our needs come from outside of us - that we have to manipulate the world into giving us what we need. Not True! Our needs are energy too, just like everything else. We meet them ourselves, by creating a space inside of us for the energy to flow into. The physical forms that we see on the outside are just the end result.

Ok, let's get back to explaining the mechanics behind this idea. We go through the Growth process, claim an energy as part of our energy field (say, for instance, *love*), and that *love* begins to flow out of us every time we give any of our energy to the outside world. So, why do we not feel loved? Why is our spouse not more physically affectionate, why does our mother still refuse to see anything but our faults and shortcomings? Where is the Receiving that is supposed to be flowing back to us?

Well, if the process is breaking down, it is probably because we are confusing the concepts of Energy and Form again. If we have truly claimed that energy and are letting it flow out in our Giving, then that energy **is** out there and is **trying** to flow back to us. Our job is to not block that flow by getting hung up on a particular form. Our world may be filled with people showering us with *love* and we cannot see it because, damn it!, it **should** come back to us through those closest to us. People are Forms. Our mother is a Form. Our spouse is a Form. If we are trying to force the energy to come back to us through a particular vehicle (Form) then we are strangling the flow.

Now it may be that our mother has not claimed much of the energy of *love* for herself, and the space it occupies in her energy field is very small. If mother's Giving space is so small that she is incapable of giving us all the *love* we need, then we are abusing ourselves by insisting that her space is the **only** place we can receive from. If we can't get beyond a particular Form being a **must** or a **should**, there may be another "lesson" present that we need to go back and tackle through the Growth Cycle. Remember Growth and Manifestation are a self-correcting and self-perpetuating cycle. We have to avoid the temptation to get attached to particular Forms, even if there is a "perfect" form that seems like it would fit the bill wonderfully and why, oh, why is it not working out like I want???! You've run across some of those, haven't you?

Additionally, we can often fixate on the **way** in which we want to Receive. These are Forms too.

Perhaps our mother **is** giving us all the *love* we are putting out, but the only way she is capable of giving *love* is by cooking wonderful meals for us. But we don't want that! That is not the **way** (Form) that we want that *love* to come to us. Our real need is an **Energy.** The Form that it comes back to us in will not change the Energy. The Energy of *love* is still the same energy whether it is in the Form of home-baked cookies or eloquently written declarations of undying affection. Our need for *love* will still be met. If we let it. Remember: needs are energy and not "things." If we believe that one "thing" is better at meeting our need than another, then we still have an attachment to that particular Form and we need to go back through the Growth Cycle and see what statement that is making about who we are. Our attachment to this particular Form is what prevents us from trusting that it is the Energy which will satisfy us. Perhaps our spouse is totally devoted and loving, but some block (lesson) is preventing them from expressing that part of themselves in the Form of physical affection. If we can't let go of our attachment to that particular form, then we will block ourselves from receiving what they have to give. If this occurs, then there is probably still a lesson there for us as well as for them. These attachments to Forms sabotage us in other ways as well.

Pouring all our energy into a certain Form that can't or won't give back to us is a tremendous drain. And we may, in fact, be consciously aware of how unsatisfying the situation is, but we get so afraid that our needs won't be met, that we can't let go. This particular form, whatever it may be, has worked so well for us in the past, we begin to feel that **only** that form can meet our need. Not True! Our needs are really Energy. The Forms are just the vehicles.

This does not mean that we can't ask for a particular form that we like. We can say to our spouse: "I need *love,* and physical affection is a way of showing that *love* which I know I would be able to receive very well....Do you think you would be able to support me in this way?" Maybe they say yes, maybe they say no. Either way the focus has been taken off the Form and placed on the Energy. Now, if we try many different forms and that particular relationship just doesn't seem capable of meeting **any** of them, then there probably is no Energy flowing back to us through that avenue and we would be foolish and self-abusive not to open ourselves up to another avenue. If we are Giving it out, that

Energy **wants** to come back to us somehow. Just as water wants to flow into the space left behind when earth is removed from a hole in the river bank. So does our empty space get filled. Our job is simply not to block it by getting attached to the Forms.

Forms are the tools of free choice for humans. My expression of the Universal energy of *love* may look quite different from yours because of the Forms I choose to express it through. That doesn't mean my form is better than yours. If I seem to be more capable of expressing that energy than someone else, it probably just means I have opened up a bigger space for that energy.

Each time we successfully negotiate the Giving and Receiving Cycle, our space for that particular energy gets bigger. Likewise, whenever we pour our energy into a form or situation that does not give back to us equally, our space gets smaller.

This phenomenon of shrinking space is particularly dangerous because it is often the original reason that we establish the blocks in our energy field which lead to our creating things we don't want. For instance: as a child, Judy gets attached to the Form of receiving the energy of *acceptance* from her father. Her father is a crusty old type that can't say a positive thing about anyone, so Judy pours all her energy into this form to no avail. No matter how much energy she puts forth, she receives little or no *acceptance* from her father. She has put out all this energy, and none has been allowed to come back into that space left behind. Remember, Nature abhors a vacuum. Like the stomach of a person on hunger strike, her space begins to shrink. Soon an Untruth begins to form – "I am not worthy of *acceptance*." "I've tried and tried and not gotten it; not being worthy is the only possible explanation."

If this block stays in place, Judy will manifest situations throughout her life in which - sure enough - she is not accepted for who she is. The Untruth blocks her from holding the energy of *acceptance* in her Heart chakra. And since she is not sending the energy out, no space is created for it to flow back to her. You've seen people like this, haven't you? They work like a dog for a boss who treats them terribly. They stay up all night to finish a report, while taking care of a sick child, and get no thanks. When you point this out, they invariably say something like "Oh, that's just part of the job, I can't expect him to understand my situation."

If Judy has tried to voice her dissatisfaction with this situation to her father and gotten no response, or a negative one such as punishment, she may also internalize the Untruth: "There is no room in this world for me to voice who I am and what I'm going through." In later life when her boss treats her badly, she may say to herself: "It won't do any good to say anything – he won't listen." Even though this powerlessness may cause her endless frustration and hurt – to the point that it becomes a constant raw wound that never heals – she sticks with that Untruth because she believes it is "just the way the world works."

Why did Judy attach to this particular form? Why, when her Giving and Receiving Cycle broke down, did she internalize this failure into an Untruth? Other people have been in the same situation and not reacted that way. Well, who can say why this happened? Maybe Judy never resolved this issue in a past life (if you believe in that). The point is that, even though, on some level, Judy made a choice to believe these Untruths absolutely, that choice is probably not one she would have made with her own best interest in mind. She, and most of the rest of us, would, if given a chance to see both of her options side-by-side, have little difficulty in choosing the real Truth of Perfection. "Hm, let's see, being part of the same energy as God/Perfection – powerful, worthy, perfect in every way – or being frustrated, powerless, and unable to find acceptance of who I am in any aspect of my life." Obviously not a tough choice! And yet, these Untruths do get in there.

Our focus then, should not be on judging ourselves for having chosen "badly" or being stuck in some "lesson" and never seeming to make progress, but it should be on being aware of those "hurt" places in our life where we have allowed no space for change to come in....and healing them.

As we saw in the Growth Cycle, change occurred only when an Untruth was recognized and moved out, and a Spiritual quality (energy) was moved into that space. The Giving and Receiving Cycle is also focused around this idea of creating a space in your energy field and filling that space with the appropriate energy. When you get right down to it, this idea is the crux of this whole book – if everything is energy, there can be no change unless a space is created for a new energy to move into our fields. No movement of energy = a stagnant life.

This process of becoming Aware of our hurt places, moving out the Untruth that caused them, claiming some facet of our Truth (Perfection) to replace it, manifesting it into our Physical reality and also into our give-and-take with the Universe is, in the broadest sense, the process of healing. This sweeping panorama I have just described really encompasses all the Cycles and information that we have covered in this book. Thus, by turning our attention now to the subject of healing, we can recap and tie up any loose ends.

# 6

# *Healing*

All healing is really self-healing. If a medical doctor stitches up a deep gash and treats it with antibiotic ointment, she is not healing it. She is creating a climate in which the body in question can heal itself without the outside interference of infection. That is all any healer can do, be they Chinese herbalist or AMA surgeon. Each is sending out the energy of *healing* (yes, healing is an energy just like everything else) through whatever forms they understand and believe in – gingko tree bark or surgical tumor removal – but the choice to open up a space to receive that energy is still in the hands of the recipient. As is the original choice to believe the Untruth that caused the problem.

But what about a psychic healer or a miracle-preacher who has a direct line to God? Can't they "see" the block in my "aura" and just reach right in to my energy field and take it out? Yes, maybe, but unless you have chosen to change, on some level, the problem will just be created all over again. Let's go back to our fictional character, Judy, and follow the process all the way through.

Judy, when we last left her, had internalized the Untruths: " Who I am is not worthy of *acceptance*" and "There is no room in this world for me to voice who I am and what I'm going through." Yuck! Double Whammy! Basic translation: I can't accept good things in to my life, and I'm powerless to change that.

The energy center for Power and Communication in our fields is the Throat chakra located in our necks. Judy's interlocking set of Untruths has set up a pattern that doesn't allow much energy to flow through hers. So when situations where she feels powerless and not heard come up, she can not easily express the hurt and frustration that she feels. The words seem to "get stuck in her throat."

For instance: Judy's husband (let's call him Paul) is a very sweet guy, but he is also a man who has trouble acknowledging his feelings. Emotions scare Paul, and the less he has to do with them the better. So Judy tries to talk to him about their relationship and share how she feels about where they are going. Of course, Paul doesn't want to hear any talk of feelings. He denies his own, and when Judy shares hers, he tries to tell her she is being silly and "you don't really mean that, honey." Judy feels hurt and frustrated. A very important side of who she is was just denied and not listened to. She feels powerless to change, or even address the situation – the very subject is taboo for Paul.

Over and over, in many different ways, Judy tries to express this part of herself to Paul. The words change, but the outcome is always the same. She thinks about getting a divorce, but that Untruth is in there pretty deep and it always says "There is no room in this world for you to voice who you are" – so what's the use? She feels she would be in the same boat with another husband, and at least Paul is a nice guy. This fatalistic frustration is the emotion that holds the Untruth in place. Remember: all Untruths are held in place by emotion. Judy

keeps creating these no-win situations throughout her life.

Those emotions, hurt and frustration, are
energies like everything else. Are you sick of me
saying "Everything is energy" yet? Anyway, if
you remember high school physics class, you
know that energy can neither be created nor
destroyed. First Law of Thermodynamics. So, if
the emotions don't get expressed, they don't just
"go away"– they build up until they eventually
resemble the stagnant pool of water behind a
logjam. Stagnant energy manifests in the physical body as disease. So Judy develops throat cancer. After all, what is cancer but cells that are not
expressing in the normal way.

Now cancer is pretty extreme. It could be
that Judy has a good chiropractor or massage
therapist that is skilled in moving energy
through the body. With regular sessions, they
help keep that blocked energy from getting to
the critical point, so that Judy never has anything worse than a chronic sore throat. Perhaps
Judy is able to vent some of her frustration to
her girlfriends and, this too, dissipates some of
that pent up energy, so that all she ever has is
some thyroid problems. Either way, the block
never really gets taken out of her energy field,

so, for the sake of example, let's take it to the extreme and say she gets cancer.

Ok. Judy goes to the doctor and gets the bad news. He recommends surgery and chemotherapy. He sends her home to think about it. Paul gets the news and is very upset, which makes him want to run away from the situation. He resolves, though probably not on a conscious level, to take care of the situation by not letting anybody get upset. Whenever Judy starts to get afraid, Paul distracts her with a joke, or tries to steer the conversation towards "something more pleasant," or says whatever he thinks it is Judy wants to hear – anything to keep the surface calm.

This just makes things worse. Paul's emotional "care-taking" (even though it fits, I cringe to use this word because it has become one of those ubiquitous pop-psychology buzz-words) is actually snatching away opportunities for Judy to confront her lessons. He may think he is making life better for her by taking away those "painful" emotions, but he is really stealing from her. Taking away chances to grow, to heal. Each emotionally charged moment in our life, no matter how painful or unpleasant to confront, is really an opportunity to look at a need of ours that is not getting met. Remember the Growth Cycle?

This "care-taking" or taking away lesson opportunities from people, creates an energy "debt" that bonds two people together until that debt is paid, as a credit card bill connects you to that company. This debt is called "karma." You always wondered what that word meant, didn't you? Karma occurs anytime you violate another being's free will – their right to choose, even if it's the "wrong" choice! It figures very prominently in any discussion of reincarnation or past lives, but that is a topic beyond the scope of this book. Suffice it to say, we all probably create enough things for ourselves to work on without going looking for trouble, right?

The flip-side of this care-taking issue is that whenever you express some **real** part of who you are, and the other person gets upset – guess what? – you just created an opportunity for them. Don't feel guilty, pat yourself on the back. If you're just being mean, that is not part of your real Truth.

But we need to go back and save Judy. The road to recovery for her, if there is to be one, starts with Awareness. First, she must get Paul off her back and begin to be aware of her emotions around this cancer issue. The Emotional body is our teacher. Our emotions tell us if we have a need not being met, and, if we can sit with them long enough, they will take us right to the block (Untruth) that is causing the problem. Whenever you are at a loss for how to begin changing a situation, you can always get the ball rolling by asking yourself, "What am I feeling?"

So Judy begins checking in with her feelings and speaking about them in her cancer support group. Now it may take awhile for Judy to find that emotional voice. She may have ignored that voice for so long that the first time she is asked to share in her support group, she can honestly say "I have no idea how I'm feeling." She may spend a month trying to meditate and hear only her Physical body voice saying "I'm hungry, how much longer do I have to sit here?" Or her Mental voice judging her: "This is a waste of time, why are we doing this?" But, that Emotional voice is still in there and soon, if she is willing to listen, it will begin to tell her about how this cancer makes her feel scared, powerless and frustrated.

At first she is tempted to run away. After all, who wants to spend all their time sitting in a space filled with "negative" emotions? But as she sticks with it, those feelings about the cancer lead her to the related, underlying feelings about her father and, eventually, to the underlying beliefs she holds about her own worth and power.

When she finally has this breakthrough and makes this connection, Judy wants to confront her father, but unfortunately he has already died. However, Judy's therapist reminds her that our lives are really about us, and the important thing is that she express her revelation **for** her, not to make some sort of impression on the other person. She encourages Judy to write it all down in a letter. Judy does this and reads the letter out loud at her father's grave site. Saying it out loud brings the Throat chakra into play and empowers it.

In her letter, Judy uses such affirmations as: "I am part of the light of God; I am perfect in every way and am worthy of acceptance and health; I am a powerful creator of my own reality; I have the right to express who I am into the world." If we go back to the chapter on Growth, we can see that all Judy is doing here, in her own way, is taking her Untruth into her Spiritual center (Heart chakra) and finding the appropriate energies of *power* and *acceptance* to replace that Untruth. Those energies were there all along, she had just covered them up. Those energies are part of her natural birth-right as an energy being made of the same stuff as Perfection. Exposing the Untruth for what it was and bringing it into her Heart space automatically drew those appropriate energies to the surface for Judy to claim them.

Now, *power* and *acceptance* may be so totally alien to Judy at first that she has a hard time claiming them as her own. She may have to work consciously at breaking those patterns for awhile: "You shouldn't have gone out of your way for me - Wait! What am I saying? – Yes I do deserve that!" But once she does fully claim those energies, they will become part of who she is and will begin expressing out into the world with everything she does, and thus coming back to her as well. On a very fundamental level, who she is will have changed. She will be a new person and new people live in new worlds. So the world around her starts changing to accommodate this new person. We may think that change occurs through what we do, but it really occurs because of who we are.

Judy is now powerful, and that begins to reflect in the world around her. Her boss promotes her. He never thought that she was forceful enough to be a manager, but the way she has been acting lately wins him over. Judy has also claimed the energy of *acceptance* – she accepts who she is. Judgments from her mother-in-law and co-workers that used to cut her to the bone, now roll off her like water off a duck's back. I could list many more situations, but I'm sure you are beginning to see how sweeping this change is. But what about that lump of cancerous tissue in her throat, how does she bring this healing all the way down into the Physical?

Judy has healed the hurt behind the disease – erased the smear on her blueprint that led to this cancer being created, but that doesn't mean the cancer just went away. Now the cancer certainly won't come back, as long as Judy doesn't forget this new piece of who she is, but if you remember our Law of Thermodynamics, you know that energy doesn't just "go away." So what does Judy do to complete the healing?

Well, here is where the Choice of Forms comes in. How does Judy powerfully create her new reality of perfect health? Does she go with the surgery and chemotherapy or does she do an alternative medicine like studying in a monastery where she learns to visualize the tumor shrinking each day until it is gone? That's up to her. She may do both. Both are valid Forms to carry out the underlying energy. We very often fall into separate, warring camps debating an issue like this. New Age vs. the AMA! The truth is that the Forms are not important; the Energy is. Which ever Form Judy believes is the most effective, is the one she will be able to best channel her energy through.

We see then that Healing is part and parcel of Growth. That the Manifestation of Physical healing is just the end result of a change that has already taken place when we open up a space in our energy fields for a new energy to come in.

Taking that a step further, we can see that every situation that has an emotion attached (and remember they all do!) is an opportunity. An opportunity for us to celebrate supported by a positive emotion, and thus affirm and empower our Truth. Or if it is a negative emotion, it is an opportunity to discover an Untruth and thus claim a new part of ourselves. Every moment of every day can be a chance to refine our energy field closer and closer to Perfection. If we are willing to work that hard and be that Aware.

If each energy that we claim (*Love, Power, Wisdom, Healing, Acceptance*, or any of the others) is just another frequency, another color in the spectrum as it were, then our final goal is to have complete expression of all the colors...to have all the shades present that are necessary to form pure, white light. If we are ever able to claim all the possible energies, then we will have Grown to the point of Perfection/Oneness with God/Nirvana.

Now, here is the most important part. If we are all part of the same energy and everything is connected, then when I claim a new part of myself – I am not only healing my own hurt, but, in some small way, I am contributing healing to the Universe. I am adding my light and making that particular color of the spectrum a little brighter, and perhaps a little easier to see for some other soul striving for the same healing. If we are all connected on some level to the same Consciousness, then the best thing you can do to heal the world is heal yourself. Doesn't the way our individual creations come together to form the creations of a Society show this? This is a towering idea, but it is really no more than the logical extension of the basic premise of this book – everything is energy.

Furthermore, if we, and everything else, are nothing more than different frequencies of the same energy, then keeping even one shade of that color from expressing is to diminish yourself and thus the world. So the less bad (stagnation, lack of Growth) that you put up with in your life, the more good you do for the world. If you want to change the world, use the information in this book to work on yourself. Thank you.